stalactites

stalagmites

sandstone pillars

some strange rock shapes

stack

perched block

earth pillars

Prepared and revised for the United States

Teacher Advisory Panel:

Valerie Jameson, Creative Teaching Workshop, New York City,
Patricia Sherman and Marsha Carlin, The Children's Center, Tenafly, New Jersey,
Angie Finn, Community School 30, New York City.

Editorial Consultant: Sylvia Van Sickle

U.S.A. Edition 1975
Macdonald Educational, 850 Seventh Avenue, New York, N.Y. 10019

Library of Congress Catalog Card Number 75-19982

Printed and Bound in Great Britain

MACDONALD FIRST LIBRARY

Rocks and Mining

Macdonald Educational
350 Seventh Avenue
New York
N.Y. 10019

The earth we live on is covered with rocks.
These rocks cannot usually be seen.
They are underneath the grass and soil.
But the rocks can almost always be seen beside the sea.
Even the sand beside the sea is really tiny pieces of rock.

Look at this piece
of rock.
It has different
colors.

granite

A rock is made of things
called minerals.
The colors you see in
this rock are the
different minerals.

This rock is a kind
called granite.
Granite is a very
hard rock.
It is good for
making buildings.

Long ago the earth was a burning ball of gas.
Slowly it became cool.
The gas turned into a runny liquid.
Then the outside grew hard and turned into rocks.
The rocks made a crust around the earth.
But deep down inside the earth, it is still hot.

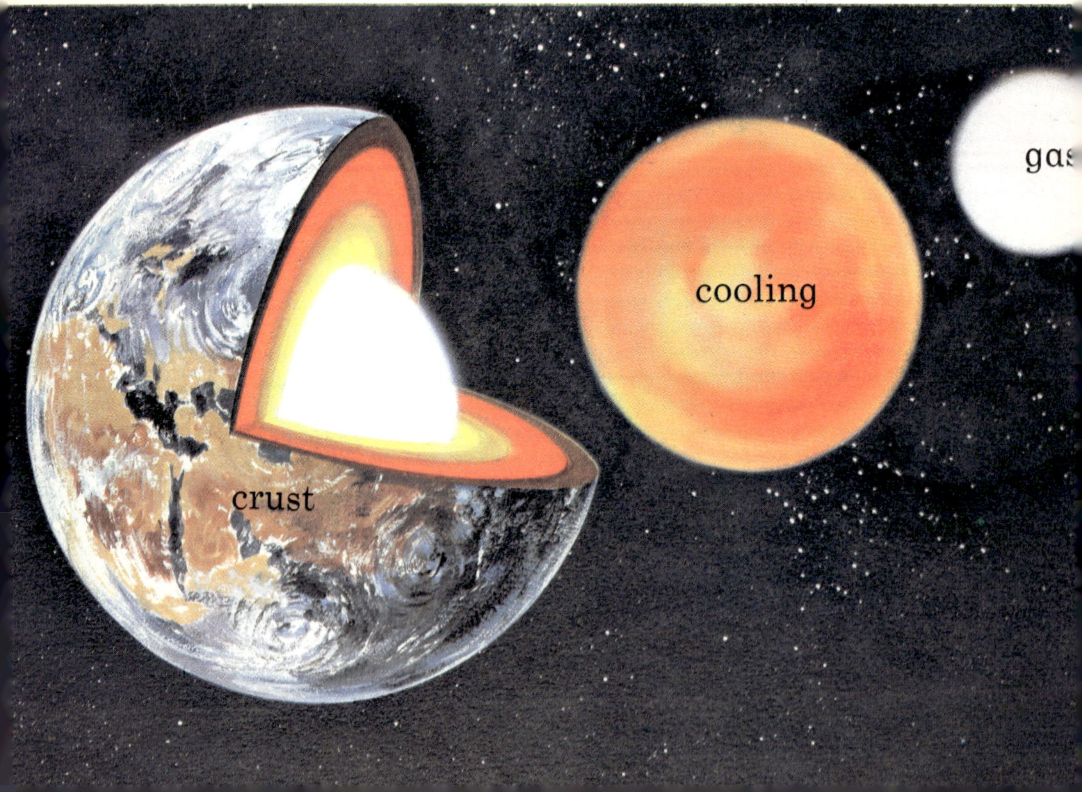

These first rocks are called igneous rocks. Igneous means made by fire.

Volcanoes make igneous rocks.

Hot lava sometimes bursts out of them and hardens into rock.

Other rocks are made by weather.
Wind, rain and snow hit the igneous rocks.
After many years the rocks are broken into little pieces.
Rivers and snow wash the pieces into seas and lakes.
Wind blows other pieces in after them.
Under the water the pieces are crushed together and become rocks again.

The little pieces are piled on top of each other like layers in a cake.
Each layer is called a sediment.
Rocks made like this are sedimentary rocks.

Shale is a sedimentary rock.
You can clearly see the layers in it.

sedimentary rocks

Sometimes the earth's crust moves.
Parts are pushed deep down into the earth.
It is very hot deep inside.
The heat melts the rocks.
They change into new kinds of rock.
The new rocks are called metamorphic rocks.
Metamorphic means changed to a new kind.

Metamorphic rocks can be made from igneous or from sedimentary rocks. Gneiss is made from the igneous rock granite. Heat turned the granite into gneiss.

Quartzite is made from sedimentary sandstone.

Marble is made from limestone.

Slate is made from shale.

Rocks are made from minerals.
Each mineral is different.
Three minerals can be seen in granite.
They are called feldspar, quartz and mica.
See how different they are.
But together they make a rock.

barite

pyrite

strontianite

blue calcite

some mineral crystals

apatite

graphite

Some minerals make
shapes called crystals.
Each mineral has its
own crystal shape.
There are many strange
shapes of crystals.
Here are a few of them.

dolomite crystals

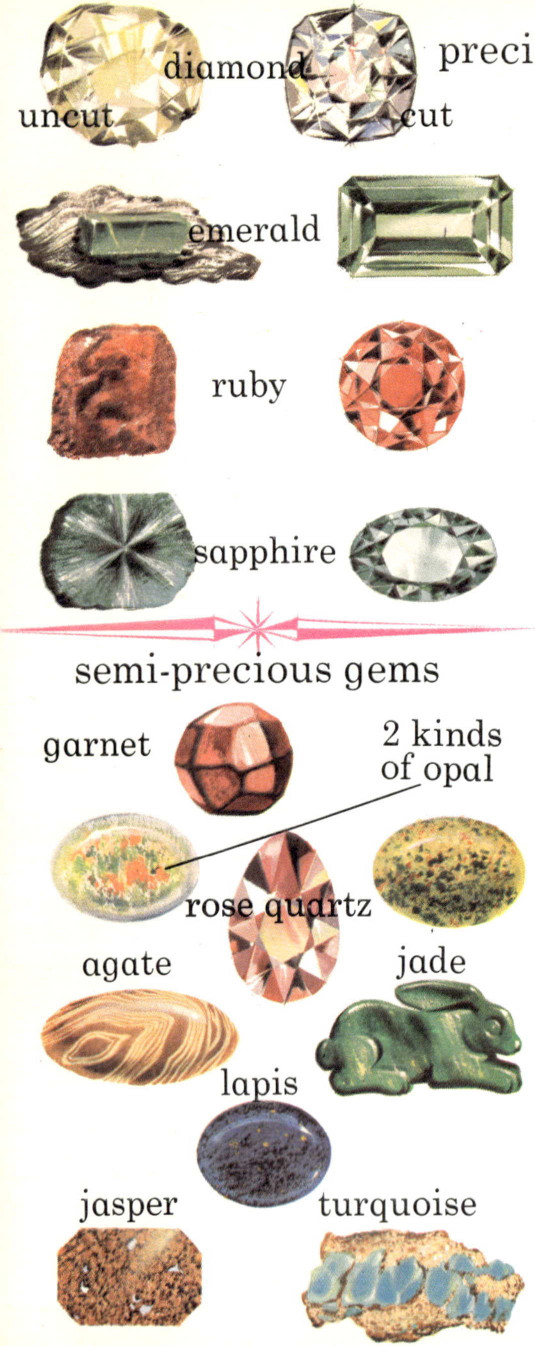

Some mineral crystals are cut and polished to make them look beautiful. They are called gems. People wear gems in rings and other jewelry.

Four gems are very hard to find. They are called the precious gems. Precious means valuable.

Other gems can be found more easily. They are called semi-precious gems.

Diamonds are beautiful.
They are also very hard.
A special machine is used
to cut diamonds.
The cutting blade of
this machine is made of
another diamond.
Nothing else is strong
enough to cut this
hard gem.

diamond-cutting machine

Diamonds are used to
cut other hard things.

drill tip

Some drills cut
through rock.
Their cutting part is
made of diamonds.

diamond blades

There are many useful minerals.

Asbestos is a mineral which looks like little threads.
These threads can be woven into cloth.
Fire cannot easily burn rock, so it cannot burn through asbestos cloth.
These fire fighters' suits are of asbestos cloth.

Talcum powder keeps a baby's skin soft.
Talcum powder is made from a soft mineral called talc.

Talc can be used to make paint, too.

Talc is also called soapstone and French chalk.

talc

Limestone rock is made from one mineral called calcite.
Crushed limestone is used to make the cement used in building.

Big blocks of limestone are used in building too.
Limestone rock is very hard.
It makes good strong walls.
Chalk is a soft limestone.

The salt which you put on food comes from
a rock called rock salt.
Rock salt is made of the mineral halite.
Salt is important to keep you healthy.

Salt can also be used in glassmaking.

Special kinds of minerals
are called metals.
Some metals can be found
in lumps inside rocks.
They are called
native metals.

Gold, silver and platinum
are native metals.
They are hard to find.
They are precious metals.

Most forks look like
silver forks.
But most forks are not
really made of silver.
That would cost too much.

Some gold is found at the bottom of streams.
Many people used to hunt for gold.
They dug up stones and mud in a pan
and shook off the dirt.
They looked carefully at all the stones to
find the bits of gold.

Today gold is picked out by machines.

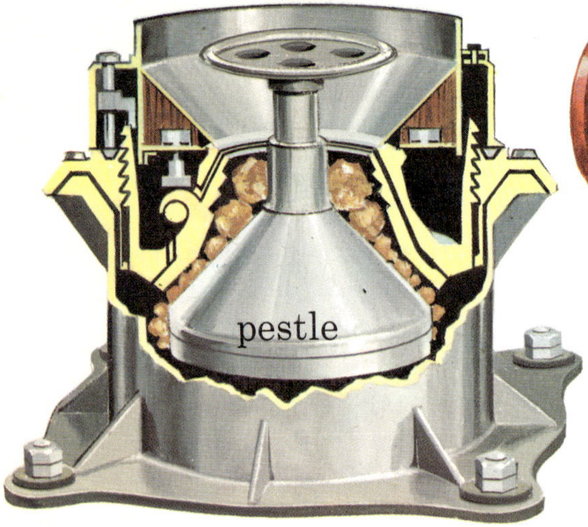

Most metals are found with other things in mixtures called ores.

Machines get the metal out of the ore.
The pestle inside the crusher machine
breaks lumps of ore into little bits.
The heavy steel balls in the ball mill
beat the bits of ore to a powder.
Then washing and heating gets the metal out.

blast furnace

Iron ore is heated in a blast furnace.

Hot air is blown into the furnace.
The furnace becomes very hot inside.

The iron melts.
It is very heavy.
It sinks to the bottom.
The dirt and other things float on top.

The pure iron can then be taken out.

roadstone quarry

Taking rocks and minerals from the ground
is called mining.
A mine above ground is called a quarry.
Roadstone is mined in quarries.
The rock face is blown up with explosives.
Lumps of rock fall to the ground.

Stone for building needs to be in big blocks. Special saws called quarry saws are used to mine building stone.

The saw's blade slices neat blocks of rock.

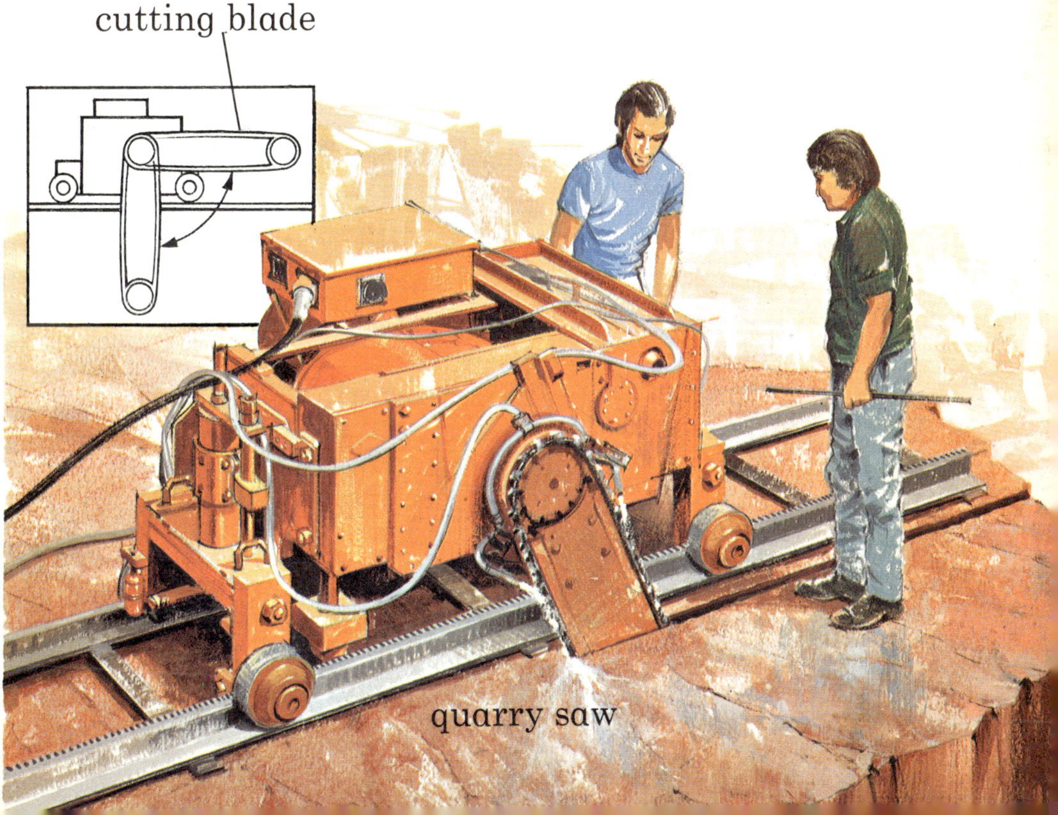

marble quarry

Marble is beautiful.
It has many colors.
Marble is used in
important buildings.

Quarry saws can be used
to cut marble.
But in some quarries they
still mine marble
carefully by hand.

cut marble block

Some rocks above ground are quite easy to mine.
Sand is really tiny grains of rock.
Sand can be quickly scooped up by a machine called a dredger.

Sand is used in making glass and concrete.

Other rocks and minerals are mined underground.
The miners tunnel under the earth.
They blow up the rock in the tunnel.
Then they bring out the loose rock.

Iron ore is mined like this.

Coal is also mined
under the ground.
Coal is a special rock.
It is made of wood and
plants which lived
millions of years ago.
The plants died and were
covered with mud.
After a long time the
buried plants turned into
a hard rock called coal.

Coal lies in layers
called seams under
the ground.

coal forest

coal cutter

Deep down in a tunnel
a special machine
cuts coal.
The coal cutter has very
strong blades.
They saw deep into
the rock.

joy loader

A joy loader scoops up the cut coal.
The coal passes along a moving belt called a conveyor belt.
Pipes sprinkle water over the coal to keep down the dust.
The conveyor belt empties the coal into tubs.
The tubs run on rails.
They take the coal to the end of the tunnel.

A map of a coal mine shows what happens down there.
One elevator takes miners up and down.
Another elevator takes up the coal.
In different places the miners are digging, cutting and taking away the coal.
The numbers show where different things happen.

Down under the ground miners breathe dirty dusty air.
Gas leaks out of rock, and fires can start.
Sometimes there are accidents.
Being down a mine can be very dangerous.
Miners are pleased to come back up to the pithead at the end of the day.

pithead

Index

stalactites

stalagmites

sandstone pillars

giant's causeway

some strange rock shapes

perched block

stack

earth pillars